Precise Patterns

Written by Claire Owen

Turkey

My name is Fatima, and I live in Istanbul with my family. We have many colorful, patterned carpets in our apartment. Does your home have carpets or rugs? Have you ever seen a carpet from Turkey?

Contents

Wherever you
see me, you'll find
activities to try and
questions to answer.

Ancient Carpets

Turkey has been famous for its carpets and rugs for hundreds of years. The earliest written evidence of this comes from 1271, when the Italian explorer Marco Polo traveled through Turkey on his way to China. He reported, "The best and handsomest of rugs are woven here, and also silks of crimson and other rich colors."

In 1905, eight carpets dating back to the days of Marco Polo were discovered beneath piles of other carpets in a mosque. The 13th-century rugs are on display in a museum in Konya, an important center for Turkish carpets.

mosque   a place of worship for people who follow Islam, the Muslim religion

Today, carpets make popular souvenirs for visitors to Turkey.

Did You Know?

Marco Polo was only 17 years old when he set out for China. He did not return to Italy for 24 years!

In what year did Marco Polo return to Italy? How many years ago was that?

Prehistoric Patterns

Rug weaving is thought to have originated among nomadic tribes of sheep and goat herders in the steppes of central Asia. The world's oldest surviving knotted carpet was discovered in 1949, in a burial chamber near the borders of China, Mongolia, and Russia. The carpet was preserved, because it was frozen when the tomb was flooded with water about 2,500 years ago.

The prehistoric Pazyryk carpet is about two yards square. Today, it is on display in the Hermitage Museum in St. Petersburg, Russia.

steppe a vast, semi-arid, grass-covered plain

Today, nomadic people in Mongolia still use rugs and carpets to cover the floors of their yurts. They also pile carpets on beds and couches, and they hang them on the walls and over doorways to keep out drafts.

Nomadic carpet merchant

yurt   a round tent of skins or felt stretched over a collapsible frame

Warp and Weft

When a carpet is woven, the warp and weft threads provide the basic structure. To begin with, the warp threads are set up lengthwise on a loom. They are usually a natural color and not part of the design. Then weft threads are woven under and over the warp threads from side to side. There are two basic kinds of Turkish carpets: those that are hand knotted and those known as *kilims*.

Carpet looms can be upright or horizontal.

Look at the carpet design on page 9. Does it have any lines of symmetry? Does it have rotational symmetry?

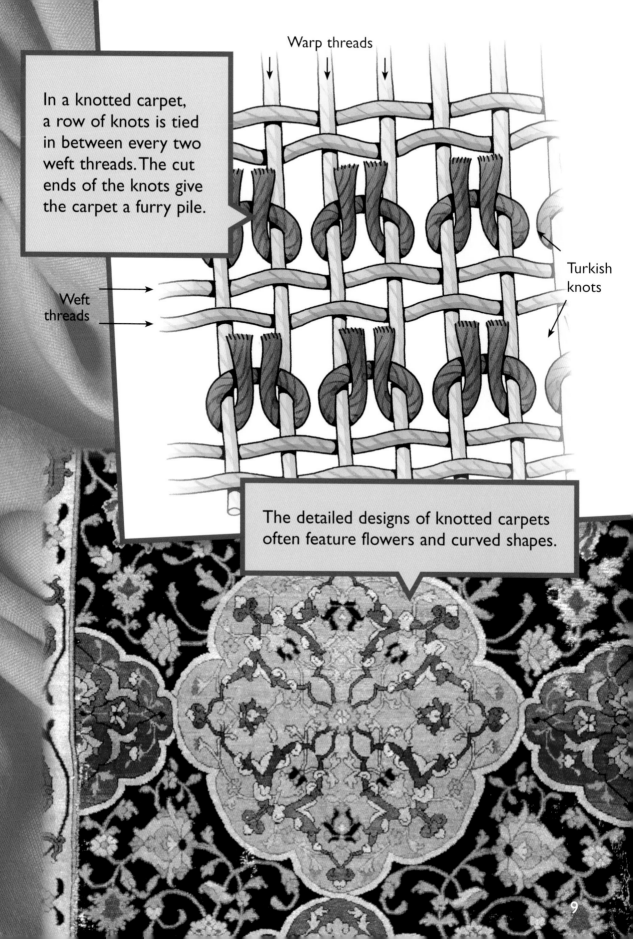

Warp threads

In a knotted carpet, a row of knots is tied in between every two weft threads. The cut ends of the knots give the carpet a furry pile.

Turkish knots

Weft threads

The detailed designs of knotted carpets often feature flowers and curved shapes.

Counting the Knots

The warp and weft threads of a knotted carpet are sometimes made from wool, but cotton and silk are stronger fibers and can be spun into finer threads. Carpet pile is made from trimmed knots of woolen or silken thread. Handmade woolen carpets have between 25 and 400 knots per square inch. However, carpets made from silk can have 1,000 knots per square inch!

On the back of a carpet, each Turkish knot looks like a loop or a pair of loops. This example shows 12 knots.

This silk carpet in the Mevlana Museum in Turkey is considered to be the most valuable carpet in the world. It has about 921 knots per square inch.

A

B

C

1. The pictures at the left show enlargements of one-inch squares from the back of knotted carpets. Figure out the number of knots per square inch for each of the carpets.

2. The Mevlana silk carpet is about 5 feet, 9 inches long and 3 feet, 8 inches wide.

   a. What is the area of the carpet, in square inches?

   b. Approximately how many knots are there in the carpet?

   c. About how many hours would it take one skillful weaver to make such a carpet?

   d. If the weaver worked 8 hours each day for 5 days a week, about how many weeks would it take to weave the carpet? How many years is that?

Did You Know?

A skillful weaver is able to tie one knot every ten seconds.

Persian Carpets

Like the Turks, the people of Persia were also famous for their carpets. In the sixth century, a huge carpet, made for the audience hall of a Persian king's palace, was woven with threads of gold and silver and sewn with jewels! When Persia was invaded in the seventh century, the magnificent carpet was cut into 60,000 pieces and shared among the conquering soldiers.

Persia the country that is now called Iran

This Persian carpet was completed around the year 1539. The carpet is 37 feet, 10 inches long and 17 feet, 6 inches wide. It has about 334 knots per square inch.

Approximately how many knots are there in this Persian carpet? About how many years would it take one weaver to make such a carpet? (See page 11 for help.)

Turkish Kilims

A *kilim* is a "flat-weave" rug that does not have a pile. Like a knotted carpet, a kilim has warp and weft threads, but not all of the weft threads run right across the rug. Instead, weft threads of different colors are woven back and forth to create the geometric shapes that make up a design. Many of those shapes are symmetrical.

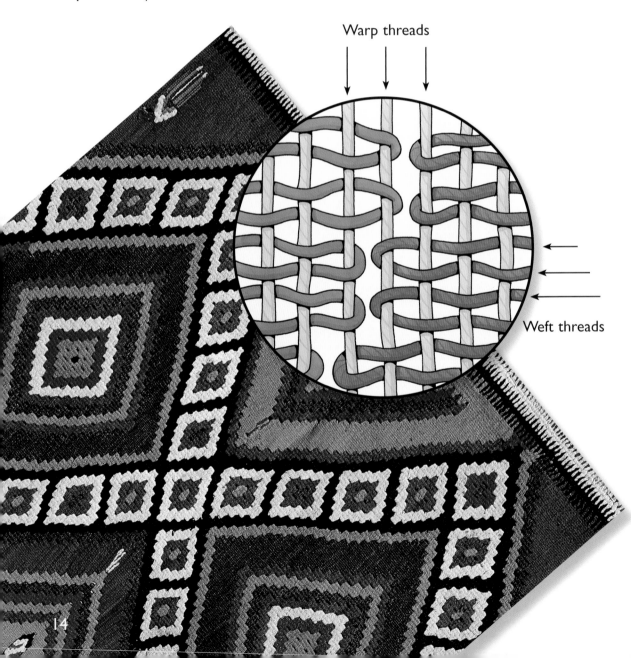

Warp threads

Weft threads

Line Symmetry

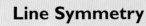

One line of symmetry

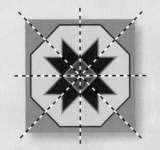

Four lines of symmetry

Rotational Symmetry

Twofold symmetry

Fourfold symmetry

Look closely at the designs in these carpets. Can you find any designs with line symmetry? ... with rotational symmetry?

15

Classifying Designs

Some of the designs woven into kilims or knotted into carpets have been used for hundreds of years and have special meanings. As shown by the Venn diagram below, some kilim designs have line symmetry, and some have rotational symmetry; some have both, and some have neither.

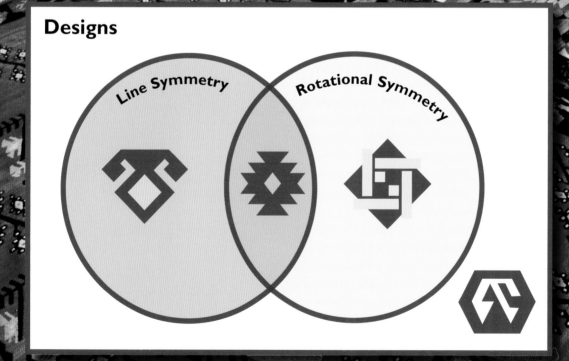

Designs

Line Symmetry

Rotational Symmetry

Classify Turkish Designs

Look at each design. Does it have line symmetry? Does it have rotational symmetry? On which section of the Venn diagram would you place that design?

Sorting Designs

Using a two-way sorting diagram is another way to analyze the symmetry of designs. Each design is placed in one of the columns to show whether or not it has line symmetry, and in one of the rows to show whether it has rotational symmetry.

Find the design that is in the wrong section of the diagram.

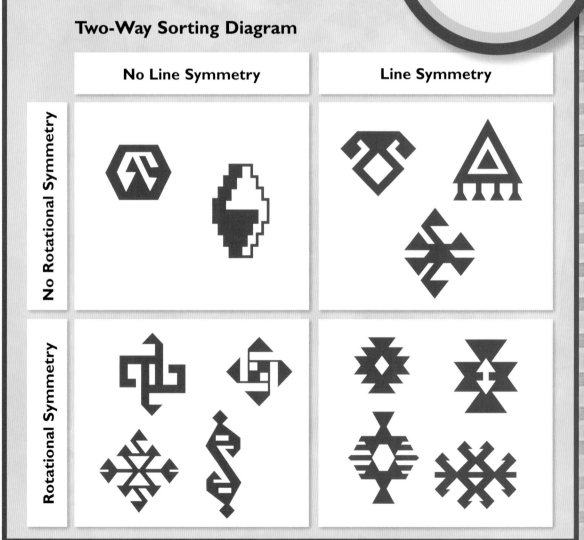

Two-Way Sorting Diagram

	No Line Symmetry	Line Symmetry
No Rotational Symmetry		
Rotational Symmetry		

Sort Symmetrical Designs

You will need a card-stock copy of the Blackline Master, colored markers or pencils, and scissors.

1. Color a design on each section of the sorting diagram.

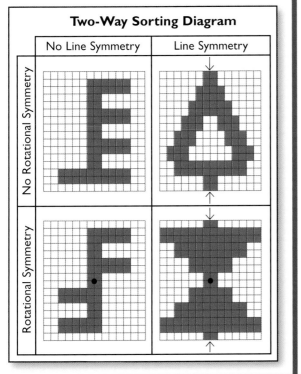

2. Cut out your designs and exchange them with a partner. Sort the designs you receive.

- Now work in a group of at least four students.

- Mix everybody's designs together, face-down.

- Take turns picking a design and placing it in the appropriate section of your two-way sorting diagram. (If that section is already filled, return the design face-down to the table and remix the designs.)

- The winner is the first player to fill all four sections of his/her sorting diagram.

Turkish Traditions

Traditionally, unmarried girls living in Turkish villages wove kilims and other items as part of their dowry, or *ceyiz*. Dowry rugs were brought out to honor important guests, and they could be sold if a family needed financial help, perhaps to educate their children. Today, villagers often weave kilims and other items to sell to tourists.

dowry   property or money that a bride brings to her husband
at the time of marriage

Large carpets are usually made in towns or cities, by teams of skilled weavers. Tourists often visit a workshop to see Turkish carpets being made.

Paying the Price

The price of handmade Turkish carpets varies greatly—from a few hundred dollars for a small, woolen kilim to many thousands of dollars for a knotted silk carpet. A good Turkish carpet will last for centuries and can be an excellent investment that increases in value over time. Carpet prices are usually shown in U.S. dollars—perhaps because prices look enormous in Turkish lira!

Turkey's unit of currency, the *lira*, has decreased dramatically in value. In the late 1960s, one U.S. dollar could be exchanged for about 9 Turkish lira. By the year 2002, it took about 1,500,000 Turkish lira to buy one U.S. dollar!

Exchange Rates

(Turkish Lira Equivalent to U.S. $1)

Year	Lira
1996	81,405
1997	151,865
1998	260,724
1999	418,783
2000	625,219
2001	1,225,590
2002	1,507,230
2003	1,504,741
2004	1,448,899

Did You Know?

On January 1, 2005, Turkey introduced the New Turkish Lira. One new lira is equivalent to one million old lira, or about 70 U.S. cents.

Figure It Out

You may use a calculator to help solve these problems.

1. Estimate and then calculate how many old Turkish lira you would receive in exchange for $250 in the year—

   a. 1996   c. 2003

   b. 1997   d. 2004

2. Estimate and then calculate how many dollars you would receive in exchange for 100,000,000 old lira in each of the years above. (Round your answers to the nearest cent.)

3. A kilim has two price tags: $400 and 600,000,000 lira. Which price would you prefer to pay in—

   a. 2001?   b. 2002?

4. Change each of the amounts in the chart into New Turkish Lira. Round your answers to four decimal places.

Sample Answers

Find out the current exchange rate for New Turkish Lira. How many new lira would you receive in exchange for $250? How many old lira is that?

Page 5   1295

Page 11   1. A. 8 x 7 = 56 knots

           B. 10 x 8 = 80 knots

           C. 11 x 9 = 99 knots

        2. a. 3,036 square inches

           b. 2,796,156 knots c. 7,767.1 hours

           d. about 194 weeks; about 3.73 years

Page 13   31,843,560 knots; about 42.5 years

Page 17   Line symmetry only: A

        Rotational symmetry only: B, F, H

        Both: C, E, G

        Neither: D, I

Page 18   (Has no line symmetry and no rotational symmetry.)

Page 23   1. a. 20,351,250   b. 37,966,250

           c. 376,185,250 d. 362,224,750

        2. a. $1228.43   b. $658.48

           c. $66.46   d. 69.02

        3. a. $400   b. 600,000,000 lira

        4. 0.0814, 0.1519, 0.2607, 0.4188, 0.6252, 1.2256, 1.5072, 1.5047, 1.4489

Index